THE PROSPECTS FOR MIGRATION DATA HARMONISATION IN THE SADC

Vincent Williams and Tiffany Tsang

MIDSA Report No 2

Series Editors: Prof. Jonathan Crush and Vincent Williams

Acknowledgements

SAMP and the IOM wish to acknowledge the Canadian International Development Agency (CIDA) and the UK Department for International Development (DFID) for their financial support of MIDSA and this publication. David Dorey is thanked for his editorial assistance.

Published by Idasa, 6 Spin Street, Church Square, Cape Town, 8001, and Queen's University, Canada.

© Southern African Migration Project (SAMP) 2007
ISBN 1-920118-44-6

First published 2007
Produced by Idasa Publishing

Table of Contents

List of Tables

Chapter

1

THE MIGRATION DATA HARMONISATION PROJECT

Introduction

The movement of persons across international boundaries is a world-wide phenomenon that is increasing both in volume and scope (Table 1). As transport and communications infrastructure become more sophisticated and travel less costly, it is likely that there will be a corresponding increase in the number of people who move from their country of citizenship or nationality to other countries. People usually move in search of better opportunities, whether these be related to employment, education, personal safety and security or more generally to improve the quality of life of the individuals or groups concerned.

Table 1: Global Migration Stock by Region of Destination, 1960-2005						
	Millions					
Region	1960	1970	1980	1990	2000	2005
World	75.5	81.3	99.3	154.9	176.7	190.6
Developed countries	32.3	38.4	47.5	82.4	105.0	115.4
Developing countries	43.1	43.0	51.8	72.6	71.7	75.2
Africa	9.1	9.9	14.1	16.4	16.5	17.1
Asia	28.5	27.8	32.1	49.9	50.3	53.3
Latin America and Caribbean	6.0	5.7	6.1	6.98	6.3	6.6
Northern America	12.5	13.0	18.1	27.6	40.4	44.5
Oceania	2.1	2.6	3.0	4.8	5.1	5.0
Europe	14.2	18.8	21.9	49.4	58.2	64.1
The Russian Federation	-	-	-	11.5	11.9	12.1
Source: World Migrant Stock, 2006 Revision Population Database, UN ESA.						

International migration is usually divided into two broad categories; namely voluntary and involuntary or forced. Within these two broad categories, people who cross borders are divided into several groups, usually defined as follows:

Voluntary

Migrants: persons who temporarily relocate to a country other than their normal country of residence.

Immigrants: persons who permanently relocate to a country other than their normal country of residence (incoming).

Emigrants: persons who permanently relocate to a country other than their normal country of residence (outgoing).

Involuntary or Forced

Refugees: persons who have left their home country owing to a well-founded fear of persecution or threat and who have been granted legal protection in terms of international and/or domestic law.

Asylum Seekers: persons who have left their home country owing to a well-founded fear of persecution or threat and who have applied for legal protection in terms of international and/or domestic law and are awaiting the outcome of their application.

Persons who cross international boundaries legally are usually issued with a permit that confers upon them specific rights and responsibilities.

As part of an attempt to regulate the movement of persons into their countries, all governments have developed systems of recording movement, primarily by collecting biographical information about travellers together with details about the purpose and length of their travel.[1] The details recorded and the extent to which such records become useful varies from country to country, but at a minimum, all countries keep some records about the entry and exit of foreigners and, in most cases, of citizens and permanent residents as well.

Despite its widespread and common occurrence, cross-border migration is often regarded as a problematic phenomenon and many governments put considerable resources and time into attempting to monitor and control who enters and leaves their countries. While such controls may indeed be necessary, government responses to migration flows are often based on perception and inference, rather than any substantial knowledge about, or insight into the extent, scope and impact of migration.

There is an increasing body of knowledge that suggests that attempts by governments to control the movement of persons, which usually involves stricter controls and enforcement, only results in migration being driven underground.[2] The emerging phrase amongst migration theorists, researchers and policy-makers is "migration management", a term that suggests that instead of trying to control or restrict the legal movement of persons, governments would be well-advised to develop strategies to manage or facilitate legal migration.[3]

Developing a managed migration system requires, firstly, a fundamental shift in the orientation of the migration policies of most governments. Secondly, migration by its very nature requires co-operation between governments if it is to be managed successfully and this depends upon a substantial degree of consistency between the migration policies and legislation of various governments. However, for as long as migration policy is developed on the basis of speculation and perception, it is unlikely that any significant shift in the orientation of migration policies will take place. Given the negative sentiments often directed at foreigners, governments are more likely to err on the side of caution and to continue to put in place restrictive policies and systems.

The member states of the Southern African Development Community (SADC), while wanting to promote regional co-operation and co-ordination and implement a Protocol on the Facilitation of Movement of Persons, admit that they have insufficient data and information on which to base and develop a workable set of migration policies applicable to most or all countries in the region. Not only do individual member states find it difficult to collect and process the data relating to entries and exits at their own ports of entry, but comparing this data between and amongst countries is also proving a substantial challenge. It is for these reasons that the Migration Data Harmonisation Project (MDHP) was initiated by the Southern African Migration Project (SAMP) at the request of the participants in the Migration Dialogue for Southern Africa (MIDSA) process.

MIDSA Priorities

The Migration Dialogue for Southern Africa (MIDSA) Process is a regular inter-governmental meeting that was inaugurated in Mbabane, Swaziland in November 2000. It provides opportunities for government representatives from all SADC member states to participate in workshops at which migration and migration-related matters are discussed and at which recommendations that member states may wish to adopt and implement are developed. The nature of MIDSA is that it is a forum for the informal and non-binding exchange of information, views and experiences that may assist individual governments in the development of their own policies and practices in the management of migration. MIDSA also provides a forum for interaction between migration policy-makers, practitioners and researchers and is instrumental in establishing and shaping research and information agendas that are potentially of value to governments in the region.

At the MIDSA Forum in Swaziland, SAMP proposed two projects be undertaken under the rubric of 'migration harmonisation in SADC.' The first project was a comparative analysis of the immigration policies and legislation of SADC member states.[4] The second project focuses specifically on the collection, processing and analysis of migration data, information and statistics. The MDHP sought to:

- Describe the data collection systems in use in each SADC country, including a breakdown of the nature of the data collected;

- Provide an overview of data processing and analysis in each country by identifying the institutions involved and the extent of their involvement;

- Comment on the availability and accessibility of data, either to the general public or specialised institutions;

- Provide a general assessment of the quality of migration data in each country;

- Submit recommendations, where appropriate, for each country and the region as a whole, regarding the improvement of data collection systems; and finally,

- Suggest ways for governments within the SADC region to harmonize data collection systems.

The longer-term objectives of SAMP's MDHP include:

- Using the information gathered to initiate a discussion about the possibilities of harmonising data collection and data sharing between SADC member states;

- Improving the accuracy of the methods used to record the number of people migrating;

- Obtaining a greater understanding of the impact of migration on SADC member states, in both countries of origin and countries of destination; and,

- Assisting SADC member states in the utilisation of migration data and information for management, planning and decision-making purposes.

Methodology

The study was conducted both in person and by mailed questionnaires, depending on accessibility, time and cost constraints. The following SADC member states were visited in person by the research team:

Namibia

Zimbabwe

Lesotho

Mozambique

Mauritius

Zambia

Tanzania

Seychelles

During these visits, interviews were conducted with appropriate officials who could provide the necessary information. The interviews were conducted using a semi-structured questionnaire that was divided into four main categories as follows:

Collection and storage of data – how is data captured, what data is captured, where does it go, how is it stored and for how long?

Processing and analysis of data – to what extent is the data collected being processed; by whom and how?

Accessibility of data/availability of statistics – is any of the data published and publicly available? In what format is data made available? If permission is required to access the data, what are the procedures used to obtain such permission? Who makes use of the reports?

Categories of data – a listing of the various categories of data that is recorded, stored and published, e.g., types of permit applications, asylum seekers and refugees, deportation and so on.

At the end of the interview, officials were given the opportunity to speak freely and to comment on or raise any issues that were not covered by the preceding questions. Officials were also encouraged to put forward recommendations for improvement in one or all of the above areas, to be included in the report. Respondents were reminded, however, that there were no guarantees these recommendations would be acted upon since implementation would be either by individual governments or within the framework of bilateral or multilateral agreements.

Questionnaires were sent to those SADC member states that could not be visited. Written responses to the questionnaire were received from Botswana and Malawi. An initial response was also received from the Democratic Republic of the Congo.

As one of the researchers was already familiar with data collection and analysis systems in South Africa, no further research was conducted there. However, South Africa is included in the report.

All told, data was obtained for 11 SADC countries, all of which are analysed in this report.

COUNTRY DATA AND INFORMATION

This chapter of the report briefly describes the data collection, storage and processing systems in each of the countries in which research was conducted. While every attempt has been made to be consistent in terms of the information provided for each country, this has not always been possible. However, the information presented does provide a good sense of the situation in each country and the region as a whole. The general comments at the end of each country section provide a summary of observations made by government officials who were interviewed or completed the questionnaire.

Botswana

The information regarding Botswana's data collection and processing systems is primarily based on the questionnaire that was completed and returned to the researchers. Tourism and traveller statistics published on the website of the Botswana Central Statistical Office provided further information.[5]

Collection and Storage

Arrival/Departure

All foreign travellers to Botswana are required to complete arrival and departure forms upon entry and exit through any port of entry.

Information supplied on these forms mainly pertains to the biographical details of the traveller, his or her passport number and country of nationality. In addition, information about the purpose, length and place of stay in Botswana is also recorded.

Visa and Permit Applications

The details of those visitors who require visas to enter Botswana or who wish to enter for purposes such as working or studying are recorded using the appropriate application forms. Generally, when persons wish to enter for purposes other than short-term visits, they are required to provide health and police clearance certificates in addition to their normal biographical, passport, nationality and residential details.

Data related to applications for asylum as well as the details of people who have been deported or repatriated is also collected.

Recording and storage of data

At the time of writing, it was reported that all data is recorded manually up to the point at which it is transferred to and stored at the Central Statistics Office (CSO), the office responsible for the processing of at least some of the data. All collected application forms are stored at the CSO for twelve months, after which time they are transferred to an archive facility.

Processing and Analysis

The data that is collected at the ports of entry and from the various application forms is sent to the CSO where, via a computerised system, it is processed and analysed for the purpose of generating reports and statistics on travellers to Botswana. This information is published in regular statistical bulletins and a Quarterly Tourism Digest. The CSO website contains information about travellers into Botswana, but the analysis of this data is primarily geared towards understanding flows of tourists, rather than other categories of migrants.

On their website the CSO also provides information about the number of people in paid employment, categorised by economic sector, citizenship and sex. This information is generated on the basis of a compilation and analysis of data on approved work permits by indus-try, occupation, work experience, qualification, citizenship of holder and so on. In addition, the CSO also processes and publishes data on the number of Batswana recruited for and employed by South African mines. The most important information source for these labour sta-tistics is the national Labour Force Survey (LFS). The Labour Statistics Unit presents the biannual survey results in its Annual Labour Statistics report.

In its census data and analytical reports, the CSO also provides infor-mation about the number of non-citizens living in Botswana based on the responses to a question about citizenship that is included in the census questionnaire. The census is conducted every ten years with the next one scheduled to take place in 2011.

Use and Accessibility

According to the CSO, the data and statistical information generated is designed to be used as a planning tool by government and the basis on which policy is formulated. In addition, some data is also made avail-able for research and general public interest purposes.

As noted above, the migration-related CSO statistical bulletins are available and easily accessible via the CSO website. In the main, these are the statistical bulletins related to tourism and the composition of the labour force by industry/sector. The more substantive published reports are available to the general public at a nominal fee. Information from the 2001 census is also published on the CSO website, but it does not appear as if any migration-related information is included on-line.

Special requests for information that is not published as a matter of routine can be submitted to the Government Statistician who has the discretionary authority to make such information available.

Categories of Data

Questionnaire responses gave no specific details about the various categories of data that is collected. However, it is apparent that data captured covers all types of applications and permits, including asy-lum-seeker and refugee permits, work and study permits, permanent residence applications, as well as details of repatriation and deportation. It is understood that, at a minimum, the biographical details of the individuals who have submitted the application or obtained the permit will be recorded.

General Comments

Botswana is one of the few countries in the region that has prioritised the processing, analysis and publishing of migration-related data. This is in part because Botswana has the infrastructure and resources to do so, but also because Botswana recognises the value of developing policies and plans that are based on reliable information. Thus, information is published not merely so that the statistics and data are available, even though this would be useful in and of itself, but because it is of value to policy-makers and those involved in developing and implementing government programmes.

Lesotho

This section is based on an interview conducted with Lesotho's Director of Immigration, Ms. Ramathe.

Collection and Storage

Arrival/Departure

With the exception of those who have border passes, all foreigners travelling into and out of Lesotho are required to complete arrival and departure cards.[6] Details collected include biographical data, purpose and length of stay in Lesotho and country of origin/nationality.

Visa and Permit Applications

Where required, those applying for temporary or permanent residence in Lesotho for work, study or other purposes or reasons, must complete the appropriate application forms that provide for the collection of more detailed biographical information, as well as information about citizenship, previous country or countries of residence and so on.

Recording and storage

Data collected at ports of entry is submitted to the immigration head-quarters in Maseru in summary form. The original forms are stored at the border posts at which they are submitted. Applications for work permits are stored by the Department of Labour.

All data is collected manually and to the extent that it is processed, the processing is also manual. Lesotho is aware of the Entrex software package that was recently implemented in Namibia as part of their computerisation, and is hoping to obtain funding and technical assist-ance to implement their own computerised system.

Processing and Analysis of Data

Immigration officials at the various ports of entry prepare and submit summary reports to immigration headquarters that provide informa-tion about the number of people entering and leaving, countries of ori-gin, nationality and so on. These reports are also meant to be produced on a monthly basis and made available to the Department of Tourism. But, according to the Director of Immigration, this does not happen on a regular basis, primarily due to a lack of resources and staff.

The Department of Home Affairs does not produce any statistical reports and while the intention is that such reports will be produced by the Central Statistical Office, this is not happening.

Use and Accessibility

Other than the monthly reports that are primarily used by the Department of Immigration itself, the data collected does not seem to be accessible in any substantial manner. This is primarily due to the fact that there is no significant processing and thus very little useful infor-mation available to other government departments, researchers or the general public. Ms. Ramathe acknowledged that in its current form, the available information was not particularly useful or accessible. There is a keen awareness, however, of the need to improve systems for data collection, processing and analysis.

General Comments

Like several other countries in the region, Lesotho lacks the resources to develop the necessary skills and infrastructure that could help in the implementation of a viable and well-functioning system of data collection, processing and analysis. Certainly, the interest and the will to develop such a system are there, but it will require a substantial input of financial resources and technical expertise to develop and implement such a system.

Malawi

Information for Malawi is based on a completed questionnaire submitted by a Department of Home Affairs representative.

Collection and Storage

Arrival/Departure

Any person wishing to enter Malawi as a visitor, for business, or as a tourist is required to present him or herself to an Immigration Officer within 24 hours of arrival and complete and sign a declaration in prescribed form called an Entry Card. When departing Malawi, the person must complete and submit a form called the Exit Card.

Personal details requested from the migrant are as follows:

- Full name
- Date and place of birth
- Nationality and occupation
- Reason for entry
- Last residential address
- Address travelling to

- Passport Number
- Place and date of issue of passport
- How many days s/he intends to stay in Malawi
- How much money s/he has to spend

Entry and exit cards collected at all ports of entry are sent to the Immigration Headquarters in Blantyre via post at the end of each day. From there the forms are forwarded to the National Statistics Office in Zomba where they are stored for three months before being moved to the archives. The forms remain in the archives for an undetermined length of time. The entire collection and recording system is manual.

Processing and Analysis of Data

All information collected at ports of entry is sent to the National Statistics Office where it is processed to produce monthly and annual reports. These reports form the basis for the monthly and annual reports that are submitted by the Department of Home Affairs, the National Statistics Office and the Tourism Department.

Use and Accessibility

All reports are for internal (governmental) use only and no reports are published or publicly accessible.

Categories of Data

Categories of data collected at ports of entry include visitors, businesspersons, tourists and refugee/asylum seekers.

General Comments

There are delays in sending entry and exit cards from border posts to Immigration headquarters for various reasons which range from a lack of postage stamps to a lack of efficient transport and delays with the postal service itself. All reports by the Department of Home Affairs and the National Statistics Office are prepared manually, which is extremely time consuming and thus reports require considerable time to complete.

In responding to the questionnaire, Malawi recommended that the entire Department of Home Affairs should be computerized to solve the delays in the processing and analysis of data. Computerizing the department would also allow border posts and the Immigration Headquarters in Blantyre to communicate with greater efficiency and for greater monitoring of illegal immigrants and asylum seekers/refugees in the country.

Mauritius

The research in Mauritius was conducted with the kind assistance of the Permanent Secretary for Home Affairs in the Prime Minister's Office.[7] The researcher had the opportunity to meet with officials from the Passport and Immigration Office, the Department of Employment and the Central Statistical Office.

Collection and Storage

The collection, processing and analysis of migration data in Mauritius is delegated to several different government departments, rather than being handled by just the Department of Home Affairs. The Passport and Immigration Office, which collects, processes and stores all arrival and departure forms, falls under the jurisdiction of the Police Department in Mauritius, not the Ministry of Home Affairs. The Department of Employment issues and records the number of work permits. The Ministry of Home Affairs has no detailed records and no publications relating to work permits.

All persons, including nationals, are given arrival and departure forms to complete upon arrival. Arrival forms are submitted to immigration officials at passport control where details are entered into computer databases. Departure forms are submitted to immigration officials upon departure. There are currently only two official ports of entry and exit: Port Louis for incoming and outgoing ships; and the international airport. Another international airport is being opened on the island of Rodrigues.

Forms are sent to the Passport and Immigration Office, which falls under the Police Department in Port Louis. Migration data is entered into databases there after which all forms are sent to the archive. Depending on availability of space, forms are kept at the archives for seven years or more. Mauritius has a fully computerized system of data collection and storage.

Processing and Analysis of Data

All systems of collection, storage, and processing are electronic. Completed arrival and departure forms are sent to the Passport and Immigration Office in Port Louis where the information is entered into the databases. This process takes between one week and one month to complete. Once a week, a report indicating the total number of over-stays and their nationalities is compiled and sent to the desk of the Permanent Secretary at the Ministry of Home Affairs.

The number of arrivals and departures is of most significance to the Ministry of Home Affairs, as it allows them to plan the size of the new airport and expected staffing levels. The length of stay and total number of tourists are also of interest and tourism data is published by the Central Statistics Office quarterly and annually.

The census, which is conducted every 10 years, also provides infor-mation on the number of non-nationals within Mauritius. The census also asks about movements made in the last five years, which reveals some cross-border migration information.

Accessibility of Data

Tourism and employment data is published both quarterly and annu-ally by the Central Statistics Office. Reports are available for sale at the CSO and are also available electronically on their website.[8] All reports produced and published by the Central Statistics Office are made avail-able to—and are used by—the Department of Tourism, the Department of Police and any other departments which may be interested in the information. Upon request, the Passport and Immigration Office or the Central Statistics Office can also produce custom reports for other government departments or ministries.

All information recorded and stored by the Passport and Immigration Office is considered public information. Details include:

- Number of visitors
- Countries of origin
- Periods of stay
- Mauritians arriving and departing
- Sex
- Date of birth
- Place of birth
- Occupation

The Ministry of Home Affairs publishes a survey of employment and earnings which contains information on the number of non-nationals employed in Mauritius. However, the primary function of the survey is not for migration analysis. The Ministry of Employment has detailed records of work permits in Mauritius, but the Ministry of Home Affairs does not utilize those records or reports.

General Comments

The Minister of the Department of Employment believes in facilitating the movement of skilled migrants in the SADC region, including into Mauritius. Creating a job bank in the SADC region for skilled labour to share knowledge and experience with other countries would help the region.

The Ministry of Home Affairs is content that their current data collection and statistical analysis meets the needs of Mauritius.

Security issues are of concern to representatives of the Ministry of Home Affairs. New anti-terrorism legislation was passed which strips Mauritian citizenship from dual-citizens convicted of terrorism acts.

Mozambique

The Mozambican data is based on an interview conducted with the Director of Immigration and several of his colleagues in the Immigration Department.

Collection and Storage

Data collection occurs in two different ways. The first is through border and airport posts. The other is via the Department of Home Affairs through its dealings with visa, passport and residence applications. Travel documents and visas are the main source of information for data collection.

Seven different forms are used to collect details of migrants:

- Arrival/Departure form – used at all points of entry.
- Visa application form – used in requesting entry into the country.
- Passport application – used by both Mozambicans and foreigners.
- Identity and Residency application form – used to request an identity and residence card for foreigners.
- Endorsement (yellow form) – used to endorse an existing permit.
- Extension of visa form.
- Residency application for minors.

Information collected is entered into a computerized database and hard-copy forms are sent to the archives where, as required by law, they are stored for at least five years.

A computerized database is a new addition to data collection and analysis in Mozambique. However, not all border posts are currently using this new computerized system because computerization of databases is still new and the change-over from manual to electronic is not an immediate process. Recording and analysis at some border posts are thus still done manually.

Processing and Analysis of Data

Data is processed and then organized into three different categories:

- Temporary (students, labour workers, etc);
- Permanent Residence;
- Mozambicans (nationals) travelling out of the country.

There is currently a trial-run publication of tourism statistics for the year 2001, which is a joint effort between the National Institute of Statistics, the Ministry of Tourism and the Department of Home Affairs. There are currently no plans to publish any other migration category of statistical information. An earlier publication of tourism statistics for the year 1999 is offered for public consumption and available for purchase at the National Institute for Statistics. The Department of Home Affairs intends to eventually publish reports and statistics electronically on a website. Electronic access to migration data is thus not currently available.

Use, Availability and Accessibility of Data

At present there is no form of public data distribution. Migration reports and statistics are distributed only internally within the Department of Home Affairs. The Ministry of Tourism as well as students writing research papers and theses are beginning to inquire about migration data. Students must write a formal letter requesting this information. However, Mozambique hopes to make certain statistical information electronically available and there is currently a trial-run program to print tourism statistics.

Data on refugees and deportees is also recorded. No other major statistical categories are kept.

General Comments

Mozambique wants to modernize its border posts by computerizing all data collection and storage systems. Modernizing borders should eventually allow for border posts within a country to consult each other quickly and efficiently, as well as afford the opportunity to communicate with posts of other countries in the SADC region. This would allow countries to efficiently consult and alert one another on migration problems or emergencies.

Mozambique feels that immigration forms should be standardized for the SADC region and that SADC should aim to have harmonised migration policies to allow for the free movement of people in the region. Utilizing a uni-visa for the region would create the necessary conditions to make free movement possible.

Namibia

With the assistance of the Director of Immigration in Namibia, the researchers were able to meet and interact with various officials in the Department of Immigration, witness a live demonstration of the computerised system and pay a visit to the document storage facility.

Collection and Storage

Arrival/Departure

Migrants are asked to complete a form upon entry and a departure form upon exit. For recording purposes, these arrival and departure forms are grouped by flight numbers.

Visa/Permit applications

Data is collected manually on index cards by surname and date of birth. If someone reapplies for entry or renewal, staff must manually look up the original application. Information is kept on file for reference purposes as well.

The completed application forms are forwarded to various locations depending on the type of visa application and place of submission. Business/work visa applications remain on-file at the headquarters, as are all applications completed at the headquarters. Holiday applications go straight to the archives. Once information has been forwarded to the archives it is stored for between 10 and 15 years.

Namibia utilizes both a manual and computerized system of recording and storage. Entries and exits are recorded manually at all border posts. A computerized system called Entrex is used to record arrivals and departures at the airports in Namibia. Entrex is a specialized computer software program designed to collect migration data.

Airports utilize Entrex to track the arrivals and departures into and out of Namibia. The information is meant to be live; which means that an entry or exit that is entered into the computer database should automatically calculate into the larger totals of incoming and outgoing traffic.

However, a trial-run of Entrex during the interview process proved that the system currently does not generate accurate statistics. The immigration official present indicated that the manual reports are much more accurate and trustworthy than the current reports generated by Entrex, given that Entrex was still in a trial stage.

Processing and Analysis

Each border post generates a monthly report of the total arrivals and departures and then sends them to the Department of Home Affairs' headquarters. However, as only airports are currently computerized, reports are not as readily generated at the border posts. These monthly reports are compiled over a period of one year and then prepared as an annual report that contains very general statistics about the numbers of travellers, countries of origin and purpose of travel.

Use and Accessibility of Data

The Ministry of Tourism makes use of the reports and distributes their own reports to requesting non-governmental organizations. Reports are also made available internally in the DHA but not publicly. Information can be made available to an individual or private organization upon a formal written request to the Chief Immigration Officer.

General Comments

Computerization of all border posts would be ideal. While manual reports are more reliable at the moment, it is necessary to understand if the fault in the Entrex system lies in poor training of staff to use software, or if the Entrex system itself is faulty. It would also be helpful to have monthly and annual reports broken down into more specific arrival and departure categories.

Seychelles

The research in Seychelles was conducted during a meeting with the Director-General of Immigration in the Department of Home Affairs and three of his senior officials. The researchers also paid a brief visit to the Statistics Office where data is processed and analysed, as well as the storage facility.

Collection and Storage

Seychelles has only two ports of entry; namely, the international airport and the seaport, both located in the city of Victoria on Mahe Island. All arrivals in Seychelles are required to complete entry forms on which they record their biographical details, passport number, purpose, length and place of stay in Seychelles and details of any tour operators or travel agents through which they have made their travel and accommodation arrangements. Upon entry, these details are captured electronically on a custom-designed system and arrival cards are then forwarded on a daily basis to the Statistics Department for processing and analysis. Once processed by the Statistics Office, cards are stored for two to five years, depending on space.

Each arrival card has a tear-off section which is used as an exit card and retained by the visitor for the duration of his or her stay. The significance of this is that, printed on both portions of the card, is a unique number that is used to track individuals during their stay in Seychelles. Accommodation establishments are required to record this number when guests check in, though they are not required to report this information to the Immigration Department.

In the event of emergency dockings to any of the 115 small islands surrounding Mahe, passengers and crew are prohibited from disembarking until the Coast Guard has received a full record of all those on board.

Processing and Analysis

Once the arrival cards are received by the Statistics Office, they are manually tabulated to calculate the total number of visitors by country of origin and purpose of visit for a particular day. The numbers are then entered into a spreadsheet which is used to generate electronic reports for publication on a website and distribution via email.[9] As a matter of routine, the Statistics Office generates a weekly, monthly and annual bulletin that reflects the number of visitors to Seychelles. The monthly and annual reports are available free of charge in electronic format, but printed versions may also be purchased for a nominal fee. There is, however, an increasing tendency not to produce printed versions of these reports.

Use and Accessibility

Immigration data is collected for two primary purposes. The first is to monitor and track visitors to ensure that they comply with the conditions of the permit issued to them. This is done by the Immigration Department using the unique Visitor's Permit Number. Seychelles courts do not accept electronic evidence, and archiving of entry cards allows for easier prosecution in cases of visa overstays. The other purpose is to develop a profile of tourists visiting the island and to use this information as a basis for marketing Seychelles as a tourist destination. Thus, there is close co-operation between the Immigration Department, the Statistical Office and the Tourism Board in the collection, processing and analysis of immigration data. All information is easily accessible and government ministries or researchers can request custom reports that are produced free of charge by the Statistics Office.

General Comments

The system of migration data collection and processing works reasonably well in Seychelles and the officials interviewed indicated that while there is always room for improvement, they were happy with the current system. In particular, they are looking at ways in which the computer system used for the collection and entry of data at the ports of entry can be linked to a computerised system in the Statistics Office to obviate the need for the manual tabulation of the data.

The size of the population (about eighty thousand), number of visitors and fact that there are only two ports of entry mean that, unlike many other countries in the region, immigration data collection and processing, is relatively easy to manage in Seychelles (as is the case with Mauritius).

Officials believe that the unique number on the arrivals/exit card that is tied to a particular individual works particularly well and it is something that other governments in the region should look at since it greatly simplifies the tracking of visitors and the matching of arrivals and departures, which many countries indicated was a major problem.

South Africa

Collection and Storage

Arrival/Departure forms

Until recently, South Africa required all in bound passengers who were not citizens or permanent residents to complete an arrivals form. This form contained personal details, country of nationality/citizenship, passport details as well as a declaration of purpose of visit. This, however, is no longer required since the passports of all arrivals are scanned into a computerized system that records relevant personal details. Inward bound travellers do, however, have to complete a customs declaration form which gathers some personal information.

Only citizens and permanent residents are required to complete departure forms that record personal details, country of destination and purpose of travel, in addition to having their passport scanned. The completion of departure forms is not required for non-citizens who are not holders of permanent residence permits.

Visa/Permit application forms

The details of many visitors to South Africa are primarily recorded via the application forms completed when visas and permits are applied for. These details are subsequently entered on the computer system and are matched with the actual entry of the person when the passport is scanned upon arrival.

As with the previous arrival forms, these completed application forms contain personal details, country of nationality/citizenship, passport details, a declaration of purpose of the visit as well as length of intended stay. For work permits and other extended length of stay applications, details of employer, residence and availability of funds are also requested.

All processed visa and permit applications, including those submitted at missions abroad, eventually find their way to the headquarters of the Department of Home Affairs where they are stored. However, now that the implementation of the immigration system has been regionalized, it is unclear whether files will be stored at headquarters or at the departmental office in the region where the person will reside.

Departure forms completed by citizens and permanent residents are captured on the computer system by the Department of Home Affairs and electronically transferred to the offices of Statistics South Africa (SSA) where they are processed and analyzed.

South Africa utilizes a custom-written computer software programme known as the Movement Control System (MCS). All arrivals and departures are recorded by means of the MCS and the system also has the ability to match arrivals with subsequent departures. The MCS is operational at all ports of entry, except the most under-resourced and remote ones where arrivals and departures are still manually recorded, although the department intends achieving complete computerization when the resources are available to do so. Recent indications by the Department of Home Affairs are that the MCS no longer has the capacity to record, track the movement of persons and generate information as required and there is currently a move towards either upgrading or replacing it.

Other Data Collection Sources

Migrant Labourers

In addition to the arrivals and departure data collected by the Department of Home Affairs at the ports of entry, the Employment Bureau for Africa (TEBA), the company responsible for the recruitment of foreign labour in the mining industry, maintains its own records. The TEBA records are very comprehensive and provide details of the numbers of mineworkers contracted, countries of origin, length of contract and so on. TEBA used to publish summary data in its annual reports but no longer does so. Primary data can, however, be purchased from the company.

Asylum Seekers and Refugees

Data about asylum seekers and refugees are collected at the point where such applications are submitted and subsequently transferred to the Department's headquarters in Pretoria. However, individual records of asylum seekers and refugees are kept on file at the office where the initial application was submitted.

Deportations

The Department also keeps a complete record of deportations that gives details of the numbers of persons deported and their country of origin. These records are generated at the Lindela Transit Centre where deportees are held prior to being deported. The deportation files include fingerprint records and are manually stored at the Department's headquarters.

Processing and Analysis of Data

All data recorded at the ports of entry is forwarded to the Department's headquarters in Pretoria, either electronically via the MCS or manually in the form of reports that contain arrival and departure information.

The data forwarded to SSA is routinely processed and published in a monthly statistical Tourism and Migration Release (PO351).[10] The report provides a breakdown of entries and arrivals disaggregated primarily by country of origin/destination and purpose of travel. While the report contains entry and arrival data for purposes of travel other than tourism from all points of entry, tourism data is limited to arrivals and departures through South Africa's three largest airports; namely, Johannesburg, Cape Town and Durban. Importantly, the PO351 release also contains time-series data, though in the published report it is usually only comparative over a period of one year.

For the purpose of submitting reports to parliament or when requested to do so by other government departments, the Department of Home Affairs is able to generate statistics spanning almost the entire spectrum of migration-related information. This includes the number of permits issued in any particular category, total numbers of asylum seekers and refugees (including how many applications were processed, approved and rejected) and the number of deportations categorized by country of origin.

Use and Accessibility of Data

Data generated by the MCS is not generally available, but can be obtained by submitting a request in writing, giving reasons for wanting to obtain such data. The decision to make this information available is at the discretion of the Department. Typically, when this data is made available it contains total numbers that may be disaggregated by any number of variables (such as country of origin/destination, type of permit, gender and so on). The disaggregation is done on the basis of the request received, but complex reports containing several variables are not easy to obtain. Suffice to say the data is available at the discretion of the department and may not always contain the detail that particular end-users may require. Data obtainable from the Department includes statistics regarding asylum seekers and refugees.

The PO351 Statistical Release generated by Statistics South Africa is available free of charge to any member of the public and is distributed routinely via a subscriber mailing list. The report is also made available on the website of Statistics South Africa which contains both current and historical reports. However, there is generally a time lag of between three to six months from when the data is obtained to when it is published. End-users may also request custom migration reports in which they specify the variables and disaggregation required. However, such custom reports are generated at a fee that can be prohibitive.

In addition to the data obtained from the ports of entry, SSA can also provide migration-related information based on census data. In the most recent census reports for example (for October 2001), there is a statistical breakdown of the foreign-born population at a national and provincial level that provides not only total numbers, but also countries/regions of origin, racial classification and so on. Recently, SSA invested in software that allows end-users to generate their own reports via the SSA website. This software will allow users to generate statistical information pertaining to migration at all levels, including municipalities. It will be made available free or at a nominal fee to interested government departments and non-governmental organizations.

General Comments

In the context of the region, South Africa has one of the more sophisticated systems for collecting and storing migration-related information. The problem, however, is that the original design of the system was based on the need to track the movement of persons for the purpose of flagging potential or actual breaches of the conditions of the permits issued to them. While this continues to be an important function pertaining to the purpose of collecting migration data, it is increasingly apparent that the availability of migration data is important for management, planning and decision-making. Therefore, the system has to be capable of recording, storing and easily generating relevant information when required. Primarily because it is stored and processed electronically, obtaining migration-related information in South Africa is not too complex, even if the actual information obtained and supplied may be limited.

Tanzania

The information for Tanzania was derived from an interview conducted with the Assistant Director of Immigration Services and the Senior Immigration Officer.

Collection and Storage

Visitors to Tanzania are required to complete entry and exit cards upon arrival and departure. In addition to biographical details, passport number, purpose and length of stay in Tanzania, visitors are also required to give details of any other countries visited in the fourteen days prior to entry into Tanzania, as well as the name of the person or institution that will be hosting them for the duration of their stay.

At the end of each day, a summary of arrivals and departures based on the information collected on the cards is prepared and this summary is sent to the Statistics Unit at the immigration head office in Dar es Salaam. Cards are then stored at the point of entry for six months after which they are forwarded to the Bureau of Statistics. The Bureau of Statistics extracts the data they require from the cards, after which the cards are destroyed. Most of the data collection is done manually, but in 2003 four points of entry were selected as test sites for a computerised system; namely, Namanga, Kilimanjaro, Dar es Salaam and Zanzibar.

Processing and Analysis

The daily summaries prepared at the point of entry contain information about the number of arrivals and departures, disaggregated primarily by country of origin and purpose of visit. These daily summaries are used by the Immigration Statistics Unit to prepare an annual Statistics Report in the form of a booklet.

Use and Accessibility

The annual Statistical Report is produced primarily for the internal use of the Department of Immigration and is not widely accessible. However, if researchers or others wish to obtain copies of these reports, they can request them from the Immigration Department and generally copies will be made available to them.

Other than being used internally by the immigration department, the Statistical Report is also made available to the National Bureau of Commerce, Tourism and the Central Bank who make use of it for planning purposes.

Categories of Data

The categories of data collected and processed are determined by the categories on the arrival and departure cards. These are as follows:

- Returning Resident
- Prospective Resident
- Seeking Employment
- Temporary Employment
- Visitor
- Holiday/Tourism
- Business
- Transit
- Others

Data and information about asylum-seekers and refugees is also collected, but as refugees who enter the country do not make use of the normal immigration channels they are not included in the information provided by the annual immigration Statistical Report.

General Comments

The Government of Tanzania is particularly interested in developing and implementing a computerised system to collect, process and analyse immigration data, but lacks the resources to do so. Initial steps towards harmonisation in the region could include:

- the implementation of SADC-wide arrivals and departure forms that could be used by all member states to ensure that the data collected in each country is standardised;

- the use of this standardized data to develop a centralised database hosted at the SADC Secretariat and accessible to all member states; and,

- ongoing consultations with a view to developing mechanisms such as a uni-visa that would facilitate collective migration management in the region.

It was recognised, however, that some member states are better resourced and equipped to begin implementing the above and that there would be a need for such member states to support others that may not be as well-resourced and equipped.

Zambia

The Zambian information is based on an interview conducted with the Chief Immigration Officer and three of her officials, as well as a written response to the questionnaire.

Collection and Storage

All persons arriving in Zambia are required to complete an Entry Declaration form in which they provide similar biographical data and details of length and purpose of visit as in most other SADC member states. Similarly, upon departure, all persons are required to complete an Exit Declaration form. These forms are sent from the port of entry to the Immigration Headquarters in Lusaka and in some cases the same information is also made available to the Statistics Office.

Once received, all forms and applications are kept indefinitely at Immigration Headquarters. If space becomes an issue in housing all forms and applications, it is acceptable to dispose of the oldest set of forms and applications. There is no archiving system in place, but plans are underway to develop such a system. All the information is recorded and stored manually.

Processing and Analysis of Data

The information obtained from the arrival and exit cards is produced in summary form and published as weekly, monthly, quarterly and annual reports. This processing and analysis is done by the Immigration Department and not the Statistics Office. It is unclear what the role of the Statistics Office is in the processing and analysis of immigration-related data.

Use, Availability and Accessibility of Data

Migration data compiled into reports is made available only for internal circulation within the Immigration Department. However, upon formal request and at the discretion of the department, such data can be made available to government institutions and academics/researchers. The annual report published by the Immigration Department is the only report that is made publicly available. Data in reports is organized by date, port of entry, type of permit and purpose of visit. Reports do not organize information according to which countries migrants are arriving from.

The Ministry of Home Affairs, Central Statistics Office and Ministry of Tourism receive and make use of the migration data reports on a regular basis.

Categories of Data

Records of migrants entering and exiting are registered under different categories (refugee, deportee, business, holiday and student). All this information is recorded at the borders and subsequently entered into record books held at the Immigration Headquarters for internal use.

General Comments

Several factors impede the ability to collect reliable data:

- There is inadequate transport on both land and water and this makes it difficult to collect data from remote areas.

- Data collection systems in border areas and at headquarters are still manual. It is preferable to have everything computerized.

- Non-electrification of border areas means that there is a lack of effective communication systems in internal offices in and between border areas. For instance, lack of electricity leads to an inability to operate facsimile machines, radios, computers and telephones.

- Arrival of posted mail is erratic and unreliable. Thus, late arrivals of forms from border posts to the Immigration Headquarters will affect statistical results.

Zambia would like to see a technical committee created to look at computerizing the whole Zambian data collection system. A technical committee could develop a plan to begin the process of computerisation at all border posts and internal offices, as well as pilot test specialised immigration data collection software. If necessary, such technical expertise should be obtained from outside the region.

Zimbabwe

Interviews were conducted with the Chief Immigration Officer and four of his officials. Separate interviews were also conducted with the Programme Officer for Refugees as well as two persons from the Central Statistics Office.

Collection and Storage

Migrants classified as visitors—travellers on business, holiday, or in-transit—must fill out I.F.1 (arrival) forms supplied by the Department of Home Affairs (DHA). Similarly, all persons leaving Zimbabwe must complete an I.F. 25 exit card. Exit cards are supplied by the Central Statistical Office (CSO).

For permanent residents no information is required upon entry, unless persons have been out of the country for over 12 months. The only indication of the movements of permanent residents is on their stamped passports. Returning emigrants are asked to fill out a form upon arrival. Other sources of information include applications for visas and work and study permits that are submitted at consular offices abroad. Details of such applications are sent from consular offices to the Department of Home Affairs in Harare on a monthly basis.

Data collected at the various ports of entry and at consular offices abroad are sent to the Central Statistical Office for processing and analysis and after six months to a year are forwarded to the national archives in Harare. The data collection and storage system is not computerized, but Zimbabwe is currently viewing different software programs for data collection and analysis, as well as looking for funds to implement a new computerized system.

Processing and Analysis

At the end of every month, embassies tally up the statistics in their possession, which include the number of visas issued by their offices. The 31 border posts (including 7 airports) are also required to send in monthly reports on total entries and exits. All reports from border posts, airports and embassies are sent to the CSO for analysis.

Information coming into the CSO is coded into categories and then sent to data entry units. Coding and data entry is all done manually. The final step is to send the data in for electronic analysis. CSO has plans to expand to a more efficient computerized system, but funding to begin the change-over is a problem.

The CSO produces an Annual Report, a Quarterly Digest of Migration Statistics and a Monthly Migration and Tourist Statistics report. Customized reports are done upon request if the data is available.

Use and Accessibility

Information from all reports are used internally at DHA, but are also sent to the CSO for further analysis. Reports produced by the CSO are sold for public consumption. They can be purchased at the office or sent via mail.

There are laws regulating which statistics are confidential and classified. Information relating to deportees and prohibited persons is strictly confidential. Actual numbers of deportees are allowed into published statistical reports, but not their personal details such as nationality and names. All other immigration information is considered classified as well, but information can be accessed by an outside source if it is authorized by the Chief Immigration Officer. The individual or organization requesting the classified information must complete a questionnaire on the reasons for their inquiry and what is to be done with the information if granted access to it.

Categories of Data

Below is a data sample summary from the Monthly Migration and Tourist Statistics report, produced by the CSO, which prints statistics on immigrants, emigrants, visitors from abroad and residents. Within each category of persons entering, leaving or residing in Zimbabwe, information is further broken-down as follows:

Table 2: Sample Data Summary from Monthly Migration and Tourist Statistics Report				
	Immigrants	Emigrants	Visitors from Abroad	Residents
Country of last permanent residence	X	X	X	X
Country of citizenship	X			
Males by age group	X	X		
Females by age group	X	X		
Males by industry	X			
Females by industry	X			
Economically active by occupation and sex	X	X		
Economically active by occupation, age group and sex	X	X		
Mode of travel and port of entry and/or exit	X	X	X	X – If departing for less than 12 months
Initial and/or final country destination	X	X	X	X - If departing for less than 12 months
Arrival category			X	
Average nights spent in Zimbabwe			X	
Source: CSO, Zimbabwe				

Details of asylum-seekers and refugees are also recorded and compiled into statistics on a monthly basis. Annual reports are produced, but are kept within the Ministry of Public Services/Labour and Social Services. The UN, other NGOs and the Zimbabwean government utilize this information. Information on refugees is available to researchers and others, but they must submit a formal request to the Ministry to access the reports.

In Zimbabwe it is the CSO that is responsible for printing and making available the exit cards that must be completed by persons departing. However, it is the responsibility of immigration officials to administer these cards and, according to the CSO, this does not always happen. Thus, information about persons departing Zimbabwe is not always accurate.

The CSO also pointed out that data collected by the Department of Home Affairs is first used internally by the department before it is handed over to the CSO for processing and analysis. This means that there is often a time-delay between the time at which the data is collected and the time it is made available by the CSO.

THE PROSPECTS FOR HARMONIZATION

The key findings of this survey of data collection systems in SADC are as follows:

- All SADC member states collect data on legal cross-border movements, though the extent to which this happens varies from one country to another.

- With some exceptions, data collection and processing systems are manual and in some of the countries where computer systems have been introduced, computerisation is limited to larger ports of entry. The only two countries that have fully computerised data collection systems are Mauritius and Seychelles.

- In all countries there is some basic form of processing of the data, either at immigration headquarters or the ports of entry where the actual data is collected. This basic processing is usually a tally of the number of travellers on a daily, monthly or annual basis, broken down by country of origin and/or purpose of travel.

- There is a significant degree of consistency between countries in terms of the data and information collected from travellers. Often this includes biographical data, purpose of travel, and length and place of stay. Less frequently, travellers are also asked to provide information about the countries they have visited prior to entry or their destination after exit, funds available during their stay and funds spent while in the country.

- In some of the countries, data collected at ports of entry is forwarded to either a Central Statistics Office or a Statistical Unit within the Immigration Department. These statistical units are responsible for producing reports that are made available outside of the immigration department in countries. Where such reports are available, access is usually granted for a nominal cost.

- In all countries, with the exception of Seychelles and Mauritius, there is a significant delay between when the data is collected and when it actually becomes available. This has largely to do with underdeveloped communications infrastructure, a lack of capacity to process and analyse the data collected, or both.

- In most countries where reports are not made publicly available, it is still possible for academic institutions, researchers and others to have access to the data by requesting this information from the immigration department.

- In terms of the data produced, in all countries there is some level of co-operation between the Immigration Department, the Statistics Office (where these exist) and the Tourism Department. Though some countries are explicit in stating the data will influence planning and marketing, there is a sense that all countries realize the potential usefulness of reliable and detailed immigration data.

- Most countries also acknowledge that a proper understanding of migration patterns and trends will put them in a better position to develop policies that are more responsive to migration realities, rather than policies that are based on perceptions and assumptions.

- While SADC states may desire to engage in a more systematic approach to data collection, processing and analysis, most countries do not have the resources, skills or expertise to put such a system in place in the short-term.

- The overall challenge to all SADC states, therefore, is how to develop and implement a migration data collection and processing system that not only assists with the in-country management of migration, but also facilitates and enhances a collaborative approach at a regional level.

The following table represents a summarized version of the current state of migration data systems in the SADC member states in which the research for this project was undertaken. Note that the table should be viewed as a comparative summary and is not intended to act as a 'judgement' of specific countries:

Table 3: Current State of Migration Data Systems in the SADC			
Country	Collection and Storage	Processing and Analysis	Availability and Accessibility
Botswana	Intermediate	Intermediate	Intermediate
Lesotho	Basic	Basic	–
Malawi	Basic	Basic	–
Mauritius	Advanced	Intermediate	Intermediate
Mozambique	Basic	Basic	Basic
Namibia	Intermediate	Basic	Basic
Seychelles	Advanced	Advanced	Intermediate
South Africa	Advanced	Advanced	Intermediate
Tanzania	Basic	Basic	–
Zambia	Basic	Basic	–
Zimbabwe	Intermediate	Basic	Basic

The harmonisation of data collection and processing systems in the SADC region is not difficult to imagine. Already, there is significant overlap between the systems currently in place in the various SADC member states and there is also substantial interest in developing some form of shared or compatible system. While the actual creation, development and implementation of such a system is subject to available resources, skills and expertise, the following are some suggestions in terms of how this might be achieved in a number of areas.

Collection and Storage

The key to data harmonisation is to ensure that all member states collect the same information about persons travelling through their ports of entry and there are two ways of achieving this.

First, harmonisation can be achieved by designing and implementing SADC-wide arrivals and departure cards that are used by all member states. This means that all states will collect the exact same information about travellers passing through their ports of entry, which then makes it easier to compare data between countries.

Secondly, and this could be done in addition to the use of SADC-wide entry and exit cards, would be to consider broadening the 'one-stop' border concept. In other words, when a traveller leaves one country and enters another in any direction, this is recorded only once as both an exit and an entry. This obviously requires a higher degree of collaboration between member states and, where possible and appropriate, the establishment of shared infrastructure at border posts. Whether forms are completed on one or both sides of the border, the critical issue here is that the data that is collected must be consistent if it is to be useful.

Data storage refers to two distinct processes. The first is the actual physical storage of the entry and exit cards that are collected. The second element of storage pertains to whether the information collected is captured electronically; either directly at the port of entry at the time the person passes through, or subsequently, when the entry and exit cards are forwarded to a different department or unit. In terms of the first process, most countries already have designated storage facilities for the entry and exit cards that are collected. However, there are inconsistencies in terms of whether the designated storage facility is just an empty room in an office building, or whether it is part of a formal archival system. There are also inconsistencies in terms of the length of time these cards are stored before being destroyed. However, neither of these sets of inconsistencies represents a substantial problem and each should be relatively easy to harmonise between member states.

The transition from a manual to a computerised data collection and storage system will prove to be a more difficult exercise. As noted above, most countries do not have the resources to shift from a manual system to an electronic system and, to complicate matters further, those countries that have invested in electronic systems use different systems. Thus, the harmonisation of electronic systems requires that member states have the resources to implement such a system and that there are consultations between member states about which software and utilities to use to avoid each member state using a separate, incompatible system. An important first step in this regard would be for member states to engage in discussions about the possibilities and modalities of implementing a uniform electronic data collection and storage system.

Processing and Analysis

The ability of member states to process and analyse migration-related data is very uneven. Most member states do this kind of processing at a very basic level by producing internal reports that reflect total number of travellers in particular categories over a set period of time. Other member states are able to produce very substantial statistical information which is then analysed and used for purposes of planning and/or reporting, particularly with regard to tourism.

One issue to consider is for what purpose data processing and analysis are being undertaken. For many countries, data collection is largely a matter of routine and the extent to which they process and analyse the data collected is limited. Often the main purpose of collecting data is to ensure that travellers do not overstay the permits issued to them. Thus, the processing and analysis of data is for purposes of enforcement more than anything else.

It is therefore necessary that a discussion of the purpose and value of the collection, processing and analysis of migration data be undertaken. Such a discussion will determine desired outputs and, therefore, the type of system(s) required to achieve desired objectives.

Table 4 below is a summary of the number of persons who entered and obtained permanent residence in Canada between 2003 and 2005, broken down by age and sex:

Table 4: Canada: Inflow of Foreign-Born Population by Age and Sex, 2003 2005									
	2003			2004			2005		
Age	Total	Male	Female	Total	Male	Female	Total	Male	Fema
Total	221,352	106,510	114,840	235,824	114,170	121,653	262,236	127,784	134,4
Under 15 years	46,635	23,762	22,873	50,915	25,978	24,937	57,603	29,683	27,9
15-24 years	33,020	14,008	19,012	35,863	15,374	20,489	40,580	17,783	22,7
25-44 years	110,560	53,995	56,565	19,758	58,165	61,593	131,213	63,330	67,8
45-64 years	24,444	11,786	12,658	23,759	12,156	11,603	28,766	15,098	13,6
65 years and over	6,690	2,958	3,732	5,526	2,496	3,030	4,074	1,890	2,18
Unknown age	1	1	0	2	1	1	0	0	0
Unknown sex	2	N/A	N/A	1	N/A	N/A	0	N/A	N/A

The table above generated by Statistics Canada is included here for two reasons. First, it shows the level of detail and sophistication that can be achieved if proper systems for data collection, processing and analysis are in place. Secondly, and more importantly, even a cursory look at this table shows the value of having good migration information systems. While only the age and sex variables are used in this table, it is also possible for Statistics Canada to generate reports showing education, income level, country of origin, occupation and a host of other variables. This provides useful information on the current composition of the country's migrant stock but can also be used as a planning tool. For example, if it becomes apparent that most migrants or immigrants are in the same occupation, the government of Canada can make policy decisions about the preferred occupations that should be granted admission in the future. Interestingly, however, Canada does not collect exit data which leaves a large gap in understanding that country's own emigration and departure patterns.

In the SADC context, with the possible exceptions of Mauritius, Seychelles, Botswana and South Africa, this level of sophistication in terms of data collection, processing and analysis is not possible in the short-term unless there is a significant inflow of resources and expertise. Achieving this kind of sophistication between countries is even more difficult, given the uneven levels of existing systems, capacity and expertise. However, this does not mean that nothing can be done to try and achieve some harmonisation of data processing and analysis.

As suggested above, the starting point for achieving harmonisation is to collectively clarify the purpose and objectives of data processing and analysis and then to think about appropriate systems to put in place to achieve these.

Use, Availability and Accessibility

Again, there are no uniform systems in place in the region that guide or determine the extent to which migration-related data is publicly available and what it may be used for. As already indicated, the majority of member states do not produce publicly-available data, though in most cases researchers and academic institutions may be granted access to such data on request. Similarly, in most member states there is some sharing of immigration data with, specifically, the Ministry of Tourism, but this level of information-sharing appears to be quite limited and, in some cases, the purpose of this information-sharing is not sufficiently clear.

As with the processing and analysis of data, there is value in thinking about the potential uses of migration data (other than tracking immigration violations) and, therefore, the forms in which such data should be collected and made available and accessible. As a first step in thinking about the use and accessibility of data, there is a need to think about who the potential 'clients' or users of such data would be. In the main, and this is already the case in many countries in SADC, the primary users of such data are departments responsible for immigration, other government departments such as tourism, labour and others, and academic institutions and individuals involved in migration research.

In all the countries where the research for this project was conducted, those interviewed expressed the desire to develop the capacity to not only collect and process data electronically, but also to make it available electronically, either via email or by publishing it on a website. However, many of the persons interviewed also acknowledged that not all member states have the infrastructure or resources to achieve this and that perhaps electronic processing and publishing as a region-wide system should be regarded as a longer-term objective.

Chapter

 4 CONCLUSION

It is apparent that there is already a great deal of consistency between the data-collection systems of SADC member states. If one were to apply the most basic standards, a process of harmonisation could be completed in no time at all. However, the over-riding question should not be whether and how quickly it might be possible to harmonise, but rather what the purpose of such harmonisation would be. Most member states are in favour of harmonising migration policies, legislation and data collection, though they may not always agree about the extent of harmonisation. However, these sentiments are based on an intuitive assessment of the potential value of such harmonisation without substantive clarification regarding the purpose and objectives of harmonisation.

It is important to recognise that the harmonisation of migration data collection and processing systems is not merely a technical exercise. In addition to the need to define what the objectives and purpose of harmonisation are, there is also the requirement to ensure that the data systems are integral to the overall migration management system, which in general has the following desired outcomes:

1. Understanding of the volumes and impact of various categories of migrants: incoming and outgoing; citizens and non-citizens;

2. Making decisions about who we want to come to and stay in our countries, for what purposes and what the conditions are for their entry and stay;

3. Facilitating the entry and stay of migrants;

4. Making decisions about what migrants are entitled to in terms of rights and services;

5. Including migrants in infrastructural and development plans;

6. Providing migrants with the services they are entitled to; and,

7. Ensuring that migration is facilitated or managed, but that it does not pose a security threat or risk.

Furthermore, harmonisation also requires that there is consistency in terminology and definitions of migration-related terms. Consider, for example, the table below and the problems it would pose in terms of comparable data systems, if the concepts and terms were not also harmonised:

Table 5: Comparison of Migration Terminology Between Countries	
Country A	Country B
Gives a 'visitors' permit to a person entering country for a period shorter than one month, irrespective of purpose of entry, except tourism	Gives a 'visitors' permit to a person entering for purposes of recreation, irrespective of length of stay
Has a category called 'tourist' permit for person entering for recreational purposes	Has several short-term permit categories such as business, research and medical for persons who are not tourists
A person who holds a valid 'visitors' permit, may conduct business, do research, seek medical attention etc.	A person who holds a valid 'visitors' permit, MAY NOT conduct business, do research or seek medical attention (except in emergencies)
Persons holding visitors permits are called 'migrants' in statistical reports	Persons holding visitors permits are called 'tourists' in statistical reports

In general terms, the development of well-functioning and useful migration data collection and processing systems is hamstrung by a variety of factors:

• Migration statistics can be simultaneously produced by two or more national statistical institutes with different numbers;

- Migration data collection is often a 'by-product' of other administrative data collection systems;

- Countries do not have the same political, social or economic interest in collecting migration data;

- There are different concepts and definitions related to migration; and,

- Data collection systems are unreliable and inconsistent due to poor infrastructure, a lack of capacity, resources and technical know-how.

The research for this project focused primarily on official data collection at ports of entry and the processing, analysis, accessibility and use of this data. This primary data is extremely useful in developing and performing statistical analyses pertaining to the movement of persons between countries. If SADC member states are able to develop systems that can sufficiently process and analyse this data, and analyse it comparatively between member countries, it would provide an important and necessary foundation on which to build and develop both national and regional migration management systems.

However, the development of both national and regional migration management systems requires appropriate policy and legislative frameworks and such frameworks cannot be developed on the basis of statistical data alone, however relevant and useful such statistical data may be. Knowing the numbers does not necessarily tell us about the causes, impact and consequences of migration and therefore cannot provide appropriate responses. There is thus a need, in addition to the proper collection and processing of primary migration data, to do further research to study the impact of such movements.

For example, if on the basis of primary data collected at ports of entry between South Africa and Zimbabwe it becomes clear that a significant number of people travelling between the two countries are female traders each country may be able to assess the impact and consequences of this phenomenon. This data will have an important bearing on the policy and legislative frameworks in each country, as well as potentially on bilateral agreements that might be put in place to manage the movement of such travellers.

Both this report and MIDSA Report No. 1, which focuses on the harmonisation of migration and refugee policies and laws in SADC, suggest that harmonisation is in fact much more feasible than is commonly believed. However, the argument must be considered that harmonisation should not be pursued simply because it is possible to do so. Instead, member states need to spend some time reflecting on the objectives and purpose of harmonisation. Based on the outcomes of such reflections, they should critically think about the systems to put in place to achieve their objectives and purpose. MIDSA provides an excellent forum for such reflection and debate.

Notes

1   S Sassen, *Losing Control? Sovereignty in an Age of Globalization* (New York: Columbia University Press, 1999).

2   J Crush (ed), *Beyond Control: Immigration and Human Rights in a Democratic South Africa* (Cape Town: Idasa, 1998).

3   IOM, *Essentials of Migration Management. Vols 1-3* (Geneva: IOM, 2005).

4   J Klaaren and B Rutinwa, *Towards the Harmonization of Immigration and Refugee Law in SADC* (MIDSA Report No. 1, 2004).

5   http://www.cso.gov.bw/

6   A border pass is a concession given to persons who frequently cross the border and who are not required to complete arrival or departure forms. They do, however, need to produce a valid passport on demand.

7   The research in Mauritius was conducted by Dr. Sally Peberdy.

8   http://www.gov.mu/portal/sites/ncb/cso/index.htm

9   http://www.misd.gov.sc/sdas/

10   http://www.statssa.gov.za/